D1562651

Unlock the Secrets to your Entrepreneurial

Brain Style

How to Open Your Business to
Productivity and Profitability

BY

LAURIE DUPAR, PMHNP, RN, PCC

Unlock the Secrets to your Entrepreneurial Brain Style

Publisher: Coaching for ADHD
        Granite Bay, CA

Cover Design by J. Kapp Advertising and Design
        Granite Bay, CA

Copywriting by Tammi Metzler
        Thewriteassociate.com

This Book is for you if:

- **You are tired of spinning your wheels and getting nowhere**

- **You feel frustrated not knowing "how" to take your business to that next level**

- **You are tired of not being able to get your product or service idea into a profitable business**

If you picked up this book, my guess is that you are either:

1. Already a successful entrepreneur and want to make sure you haven't missed anything;

2. An entrepreneur now or have been in the past and are not quite satisfied with how it has turned out; or

3. Simply curious as to what an "entrepreneurial brain style" is...and how you can hone yours to get more productivity and profitability in your business.

If you answered yes to any those initial questions and are an entrepreneur wanting to take your zillion ideas into making a real difference with your services/products and enjoy the satisfaction of having a profitable business, this book is for you. You probably have an entrepreneurial brain style!

Successful small business owners have a unique brain style, an "entrepreneurial brain style" that comes complete with an abundance of innate skills, qualities and talents that contribute to your success. Some of these inherent qualities include:

- Creativity
- Risk taking
- Being a great problem solver
- Self-discipline
- Not afraid to make a mistake
- Able to fly by the seat of your pants
- Confidence

- Optimism
- Resilience
- Good with people
- Action oriented
- And many more

Unfortunately, most business owners with this gifted entrepreneurial brain style don't know how to unlock its potential or harness its strength and therefore waste their time and energy struggling with organization, planning, time management, delegation, prioritization, focusing on less interesting details, getting easily distracted by the next idea, etc. Not knowing your strengths so you can use them to compensate or learn ways to better manage your areas of weaknesses makes it nearly impossible for you with entrepreneurial brain styles to live your passion, serve your market niche and enjoy the productivity or profitability you deserve.

Now, imagine that you could finally take those ideas and passion and serve the world as you know only you can? What would that be like? How would that make you feel? By unlocking your entrepreneurial brain style you can do all that and more!

Foreword

The fact that only 34% percentage of new businesses succeed in the first five years is testimony that it takes more than great ideas, willpower and motivation to keep your entrepreneurial business moving along. It takes knowing how to make the most of your natural entrepreneurial talents and also learning how to better execute those other, less innate business skills that keep undermining your success. The good news is that these other skills, such as organization, planning, follow-through, delegation, time management, etc., can be learned while you are drawing on the overabundant strengths of your entrepreneurial brain style.

As a certified ADHD Coach, I have spent the last nine years specializing in working with entrepreneurs with ADHD. Not surprisingly, people with attentional deficits are 300% more likely to be entrepreneurs. Their creativity, out of the box thinking, ability to come up with extraordinary solutions and knack for recognizing possible money-making opportunities make them natural successful entrepreneurs. However, they often struggle to succeed in establishing profitable businesses they can sustain. As I looked around, I noticed that other entrepreneurs, who had not necessarily been diagnosed with ADHD, were also struggling with similar problem areas in their businesses. It wasn't for lack of ideas, determination, desire, energy or motivation that their businesses were failing, but rather a lack of skills, competencies, systems or structures around those less developed areas of necessary entrepreneurial tasks.

By coaching them to maximize their innate strengths and build competencies around those less-developed areas, they were able to unlock the key to their success and finally pursue their passions, raise their productivity and ultimately increase the profits in their businesses. I want this for you too! That's why I put together this book to help you unlock the secrets to your entrepreneurial brain style...so you too can live your dream and experience productivity and profitability in your business!

Here's to your success!

Laurie Dupar

Contents

Entrepreneurial Brain Style Secrets

Contents-Continued

Who is Laurie Dupar?

Laurie Dupar grew up in the Pacific Northwest and now lives in Northern California, where she specializes in coaching persons with ADHD and those with "entrepreneurial brain styles."

Her education and background as a trained Psychiatric Mental Health Nurse Practitioner (PMHNP) and Senior Certified ADHD Coach (SCAC) make her uniquely suited to guide gifted entrepreneurs. Working with Laurie, clients are finally able to unlock the secrets to their entrepreneurial brain style and reach their service, productivity and profitability goals by creating the necessary systems and structures to better manage their focus, time awareness and organizational challenges.

Laurie's approach includes capitalizing on the unique strengths of the entrepreneurial brain style while at the same time helping her clients develop the systems and structures to better manage their areas of weaknesses. Using the same strategies that helped her earn a six-figure income in less than a year, Laurie helps her clients unlock their own personal secrets to their entrepreneurial brain style so they can create a business that reflects their passion and allows them to experience their dream business.

Laurie is the editor and co-author of the #1 Amazon bestseller, "*365 Ways to Succeed With ADHD: A Full Year of Valuable Tips and Strategies from the World's Best Coaches and Experts*" and the author of "*Brainsurfing and 31 Other Awesome Qualities of ADHD.*"

Want to talk with others who have entrepreneurial brains like yours? Visit and "like" Laurie on Facebook at:

www.facebook.com/CoachingforADHD

Find out how you can reach your business goals by unlocking the secrets to your entrepreneurial brain style at:

www.CoachingforADHD.com

Acknowledgements
&
Dedication

My heartfelt appreciation to the following people for being big believers in my dreams:

- To my husband, Dana, for his continual support.

- To my children, Graham, Joanna, Blake and Michelle, who inspire me every day to be a better person.

And, *especially* to all of my amazing clients who have taught me more about the entrepreneurial brain style than any book I could ever read! You rock! I continue to be honored and privileged to be part of your life.

■ ■ ■

This book is dedicated to all my past, present and future clients. Thank you!

"Entrepreneurship is living a few years of your life like most people won't so you can spend the rest of your life like most people can't."

~ Unknown

Willing to Take Risks

"Risk more than others think is safe. Care more than others think is wise. Dream more than others think is practical. Expect more than others think is possible"

~ Cadet Maxim

Willing to Take Risks

Did you know that the term "entrepreneur" was defined by an Irish-French economist, Richard Cantillon, in the late 1600's? According to Cantillon, an entrepreneur refers to an owner or manager of a business enterprise who makes money through risk and initiative. Sound familiar?

One of the first secrets of people like you with an entrepreneurial brain style is that you are willing to take risks more than others. This ability makes you seemingly unaware to the dangers and immediate consequences of your actions. It's this same "immunity to risk" quality that we appreciate in people who are recognized for their courage. By being focused on their goal, being able to keep their mind set on the desired results, they simply do not consider the immediate danger...just the possibilities. This entrepreneurial brain-style characteristic means that you will more likely act now while there is opportunity rather than miss it due to over-analyzing your actions.

Because of this ability to spot opportunities for growth and possibilities, as well as being armed with loads of courage to pursue these options, those with an entrepreneurial brain style will pit their resources and skills towards a desired result and typically win.

Extraordinarily Creative

"Always think outside the box and embrace opportunities that appear, wherever they might be."

~ Albert Einstein

Extraordinarily Creative

Lucky you! People with entrepreneurial brain styles invented the saying "thinking outside of the box." With an abundance of inspired thoughts and ideas that come with your imaginative mind, you have the ability to invent new concepts for products or services and use this innovativeness to come up with solutions and strategies otherwise not considered.

Successful entrepreneurs use this creativity to come up with new solutions to old problems, to get things done in a different way and to find a totally different approach for conventional things to work together. Being able to make connections between seemingly unrelated situations or events is an invaluable talent for those with entrepreneurial brain styles. Recognizing and using this extraordinary creativity is one of your most prized secrets.

This ingenuity and innovativeness of the entrepreneurial brain style is also the impetus for repurposing products that can be introduced into new markets. It allows you to think out of the box when it comes to product possibilities, marketing strategies or business decisions. Success for you with entrepreneurial brain styles may come from one single extraordinarily creative idea. I just bet someone with an entrepreneurial brain style created the "Snuggie"! Now, don't you wish you had invented that "wearable blanket"?!

Optimistic

"Optimistic: Someone who figures that taking a step backward after taking a step forward is not a disaster, it's a cha-cha."

~ Robert Brault

Optimistic

Another secret to the success of those with entrepreneurial brain styles is that you have an almost overly optimistic way of viewing the world. To you, the world is filled with unlimited possibilities...even in the face of evidence proving otherwise!

Guy Kawasaki from Apple computers has said, "You almost have to be delusional or in denial - otherwise you will never ever think of creating something new like a business."

Those with entrepreneurial brain styles not only see the glass half full, but when faced with an empty glass, they are thrilled at the possibilities of how to fill it!

Self-Confident

"People who ask confidently get more than those who are hesitant and uncertain. When you've figured out what you want to ask for, do it with certainty, boldness and confidence."

~ Jack Canfield

Self-Confident

Another key to success for those with the entrepreneurial brain style is to take full advantage of your confidence and strong belief in yourself. Use this irreplaceable quality to eliminate any questions about whether you can succeed or whether you are worthy of success.

Being an entrepreneur, it would be easy to become demoralized, frustrated and resentful if you lack self-confidence or belief in your dreams. A successful entrepreneur believes in his/her abilities and is not scared to explore un-chartered territories, take risks and make difficult decisions. Stay focused and determined and believe in your ability to achieve your goals.

Sometimes this self-optimism can be seen by others as flamboyance or arrogance and is subject to criticism. However, you with your entrepreneurial brain style and inner confidence tend not to spend too much time thinking about un-constructive criticism.

Self-confidence, however, is not a personal trait that either you have or you don't. You might have high self-confidence in one situation and totally lack in another. This is one of those essential entrepreneurial skills that can be developed by training and experience.

Go ahead and exude that confidence you feel in everything you do! Walk into a room like you own it. Dress with personal confidence. Speak your ideas. Charge what your worth, knowing that the product or service you offer has tremendous value. Believe that you will change lives. You will!

High Integrity

"If you have integrity, nothing else matters. If you don't have integrity, nothing else matters."

~ Alan K. Simpson

High Integrity

Successful entrepreneurs and millionaires rated "being honest with everyone" as the number one factor of their success. How fortunate that truthfulness, openness and sincerity is a key instinctive characteristic for those with entrepreneurial brain styles.

You live by the motto:

"Right is right even if no one is doing it, and wrong is wrong even if everyone is doing it."

Standing in your integrity, even when no one is watching, is what sets you apart. Honesty, reliability and fairness are key to your successful business relationships and success. Making sure that your business has a deep-seated theme of integrity that is evident to your customers will result in a profitable and successful company.

Having an entrepreneurial brain style, you know that when your thoughts and actions don't align with the truth, it wastes precious energy and tarnishes your services, products and overall business reputation.

Being able to support yourself by creating a successful business of productivity and profitability, while honoring your moral compass for what is right, brings true happiness, fulfillment and profit in your work. Just ask a millionaire!

Disciplined

"Discipline is the bridge between goals and accomplishment."

~ Jim Rohn

Disciplined

You know better than most that as an entrepreneur, you set massive goals for yourself and want to stay committed to achieving them, regardless of the obstacles that get in the way. This is not always easy, and one of the secrets to your success is the abundance of drive, discipline and self-motivation that comes with your entrepreneurial brain style.

Building a business from the ground up, you will most likely be faced with doing most, if not all, of the initial jobs of your company, such as accounting, marketing, web design, customer service, writing, etc. You must have the ability to get things done, even when you don't feel like it. Luckily, those of you with the entrepreneurial brain style possess huge doses of discipline and an inner drive to succeed.

You can use your self-discipline to help you stay focused on your objectives and vision in the midst of the business-building chaos. It is this secret discipline that makes you complete every task, dot every "i" and cross every "t."

As an entrepreneur, it is easy to go off strategy, and be seduced by another idea or project. It is your innate self-discipline that will keep you on the right track...or help you get back on track when temptations rise.

Making the most of your natural self-discipline will help keep your focus on making your business work, and help eliminate any obstacles or distractions to your goals. Discipline helps you to take those small, consistent steps every day toward the achievement of your goals that leads to long-term entrepreneurial success.

Action Oriented

"The critical ingredient is getting off your butt and doing something. It's as simple as that. A lot of people have ideas, but there are few who decide to do something about them now. Not tomorrow. Not next week. But today. The true entrepreneur is a doer, not a dreamer."

~ Robert Browning

Action Oriented

Another instinctive quality of those with entrepreneurial brain styles is that they are the "do-ers" verses the "be-ers" in life. Successful entrepreneurs may actually be restless when not moving. For you and your entrepreneurial brain style, doing comes naturally.

In the early years of coaching training, I remember the "oohs" and "ahhs" and nods from classmates when instructors would offer the perspective that "We are human beings...not human 'doings'...We need to BE more often." As a novice coach, I tried desperately to just "BE." I am not a very good "be-er." Like you, I have always been more comfortable "doing."

Being action oriented, I welcomed taking those small steps I needed to get my business going and off the ground. Creating my next product or thinking about what my next PowerPoint presentation might look like. For some, this may seem as though we are choosing work over fun, but "work" is often creative and fun for many with an entrepreneurial brain style.

With an entrepreneurial brain style, you don't just sit around waiting for things to happen; you go out there and *make* it happen. You are persistent and hardworking, willing to "do" what's next, especially when it has to do with meeting your goals. Harnessing this affinity to taking action or "doing" is a key secret to your enjoying business success.

Being the owner of your own business requires a tremendous amount of mental, emotional and physical energy. Tapping into this personal adrenaline source, people with entrepreneurial brain styles are able to put in those extra hours, pull those all-nighters, or meet those last-minute deadlines.

Beginning entrepreneurs may have limited funds, but they have unlimited energy!

Ability to Hyperfocus

"I do not believe a man can ever leave his business. He ought to think of it by day and dream of it by night. "

~ Henry Ford

Ability to Hyperfocus

Success as an entrepreneur means that you will have to spend hours, months or even years focusing on your business. People with the entrepreneurial brain style have a unique ability to "hyperfocus" when it comes to their businesses. You may have even been accused of being a workaholic! With an intense interest in your business, you with the entrepreneurial brain style are literally able to concentrate on one task while the rest of the world fades away. Gone are time and the outside world as you enter an incredibly focused state of mind I call "the zone."

This ability to hyperfocus is a key ingredient to your success. With this ability to hyperfocus solely on your business, you are able to notice unique aspects and develop them into something amazing. Having this focus means that you are able to know what will work best and focus on those opportunities.

As long as your business holds your attention and interest, you will be able to grab all the opportunities that come your way. This ability to tap into this single-minded determination, hyperfocus, is a key reason why many with entrepreneurial brain styles create the success we recognize in their businesses.

Skilled at Multi-Tasking

"A human being should be able to change a diaper, plan an invasion, butcher a hog, conn a ship, design a building, write a sonnet, balance accounts, build a wall, set a bone, comfort the dying, take orders, give orders, cooperate, act alone, solve equations, analyze a new problem, pitch manure, program a computer, cook a tasty meal, fight efficiently, die gallantly. Specialization is for insects."

~Robert Heinlein

Skilled at Multi-Tasking

Along with the ability to hyperfocus when highly interested in their business, successful entrepreneurs also have a seemingly contradictory quality of being a jack-of-all-trades and switching their attention from task to task if needed extremely quickly.

Especially in the beginning stages of your businesses, you are required to have many skills and juggle them consecutively. The entrepreneurial brain style, which may have difficulty maintaining focus on a single thing if that one thing is not of interest to them, is at its best when doing several tasks at the same time, especially when these tasks include areas of inherent interests, strengths and passions. By combining otherwise mundane tasks, such as bill paying or invoicing, with entrepreneurial activities such as web browsing, listening to music, talking on the phone and answering emails, these more mundane tasks are more likely to be completed.

Great People Skills

"The less you speak, the more you will hear."

~ Alexander Solshenitsen

Great People Skills

Another critical factor that you have as a result of your entrepreneurial brain style is the blessing of having good people skills. Even though most entrepreneurs are classic individualists, they understand that their success is a result of a team effort. This natural charisma often attracts liked-minded employees and helps to keep them motivated!

Those with entrepreneurial brain styles are genuinely interested and curious about people. Possessing strong communication skills, knowing how to carry on a conversation, genuinely listening to others, and being friendly are your tickets to success. With good people skills, you will be able to sell your product, point of view, idea and especially yourself.

Perseverance

"I do not think that there is any other quality so essential to success of any kind as the quality of perseverance. It overcomes almost everything, even nature."

~ John D. Rockefeller

Perseverance

Entrepreneurs, like you, possess a high level of energy, sustainable over long hours in order to make your business successful. You are tenacious, persistent, and able to dig deep within yourself to keep going. When things don't go your way, you are able to handle the rejections along the journey, knowing that your sheer determination will ride you through.

Business owners with entrepreneurial brain styles are not thwarted by defeats or setbacks. You look at defeat as an opportunity for success. You are determined to make all of your endeavors succeed, so you will try and try again until it does. Successful entrepreneurs do not believe that something cannot be done. For you with entrepreneurial brain styles, "impossible" is not a word in your vocabulary!

Passionate

""There is no greatness without passion to be great, whether it's the aspiration of an athlete or an artist, a scientist, a parent, or a businessperson."

~ Anthony Robbins

Passionate

Passion comes in huge supply for those with entrepreneurial brain styles. You are passionate in your belief that you can/need/should make a difference in the world. You are driven by your passion and desire to do things better and improve yourself, your products, your service and ultimately, your world.

When you truly love your work and your business, your passion for what you do is yet another key to your success. Work energizes you!

You with entrepreneurial brain styles have the most success when you build your businesses around something you love or have a strong personal interest in. Being passionate about your business definitely makes it easier to get through the rough phases and obstacles when initial or occasional failures are bound to occur.

When you love what you do or do what you love, you are willing to put in those extra hours to make the business succeed. Working is a source of joy, play, fun and satisfaction that goes beyond money. For you with the entrepreneurial brain style, the financial rewards simply follow the pursuit of your passion.

How you follow your passion will be unique to you. That is part of what makes you so special. Harnessing your passions, being able to use that deep well of enthusiasm, will help to bring you the professional success and the personal fulfillment you deserve.

Natural Leader

"A boss creates fear, a leader confidence. A boss fixes blame, a leader corrects mistakes. A boss knows all, a leader asks questions. A boss makes work drudgery, a leader makes it interesting. A boss is interested in himself or herself, a leader is interested in the group."

~ Russell H. Ewing

Natural Leader

Did you know that with your entrepreneurial brain style, you are a natural leader? Your unique combination of innate leadership skills draws people to you. You communicate effectively, motivate others with your passion, sell your ideas, work hard and act as a good role model for integrity, and people naturally follow your lead.

Where it gets challenging for you, with entrepreneurial brain styles, is in recognizing that being a natural leader also means that you don't/can't do it all yourself. It might be tough at times, for you, with your independent spirit or "super hero" brain style abilities to let go and delegate.

Successful entrepreneurial businesses know that the key to business productivity and profitability is finding the right people who can do the jobs you can't do, don't want to do, don't have time for or are not in your area of genius. As an entrepreneurer, you are the innovator, the problem solver, and the juice behind creating a more productive, profitable and satisfying business. Recognizing and effectively delegating jobs and tasks to others based on your and their strengths and weaknesses, is essential.

Finally, as a natural leader, you also realize that successful entrepreneurs don't know everything. In fact knowing or admitting what you <u>don't know</u> is an indispensable trait of yours. You know that being willing, seeking and learning from the advice and resources of other like-minded leaders and experts in your niche, is all in the interest of achieving your business goals.

Willing To Do Whatever It Takes

"Opportunity is missed by most people because it is dressed in overalls and looks like work."

~ Thomas Edison

Willing to Do Whatever it Takes

The desire and dedication to reach your goals through good old-fashioned hard work is another secret to the success of those with entrepreneurial brain styles. Simply, there's no substitute for hard work and a core belief that you are willing to do "whatever it takes" to succeed and become a successful entrepreneur.

I bet you are the first person to arrive at the office and the last one to leave. You work weekends and holidays if needed to make sure that an outcome meets your expectations, and your mind is constantly on work and your business, whether you are "at work" or not.

Most people are not willing to put in the work; they want the fastest and easiest solution when it comes to success. With your entrepreneurial brain style, inner dedication and willingness to do "whatever it takes," as long as you can stay motivated and focused on your goals, you have what it takes to succeed.

Unique

"A rock pile ceases to be a rock pile the moment a single man contemplates it, bearing within him the image of a cathedral."

~ Antoine de Saint-Exupéry

Unique

One of the biggest secrets to an entrepreneur's success is their own unique combination of abilities, talents, experience and expertise that sets them apart from others in that niche. In addition to your unique blend of entrepreneurial brain style skills and abilities, you have a wealth of real life experiences and education to draw from.

Not surprisingly, about half of all home-based start-ups are launched by people, like you, who decide to use their knowledge gained from previous work experience, expertise or personal interest to start their business.

Debbie Fields, owner of Mrs. Fields cookies, created a productive and profitable business based on the sense of satisfaction she got as a kid making cookies for family and friends.

Estee Lauder started her career when she agreed to help her uncle, a chemist named Dr. Schotz, sell some of the creams he made for the company. Today, Estee Lauder is a recognized brand name in over 118 countries with $3.6 billion in annual sales. J.K. Rowling, author of the *Harry Potter* series, has amassed a fortune from a childhood pastime of telling, writing and often acting stories out with her younger sister, Di.

In addition to having an entrepreneurial brain style, what other natural gifts, talents and genius do you have? Identifying your unique qualities is the tip of the iceberg to unearthing your entrepreneurial success.

Loves a Challenge

"The ultimate measure of a person is not where they stand in moments of comfort and convenience, but where they stand in times of challenge and controversy."

~ Martin Luther King, Jr.

Loves a Challenge

Competition is everywhere. And it is the perfect world to thrive in for those with entrepreneurial brain styles. Where others might shy away from a challenge, you thrive on it! Often, you will compete with your own goals and self-imposed high standards, but out-marketing and outperforming your competitors might also drive you. This standard of excellence and love of a challenge is a key secret to your chances of being a successful entrepreneur.

Challenging yourself to do a better job, produce a better product, and serve in a more meaningful way than someone else drives you. Those with the entrepreneurial brain style see challenges not as obstacles but opportunities.

Loves to Learn

"Learning is a treasure that will follow its owner everywhere."

~ Chinese Proverb

Loves to Learn

You with entrepreneurial brain styles love to learn! In fact, you are lifelong learners. One study of entrepreneurs found that 95 percent of those surveyed had earned bachelor degrees, and 47 percent had more advanced degrees in one or more subjects. Interestingly, most of these degrees were not related directly to business!

For you, your innate entrepreneurial brain style and desire to learn means that you can even succeed without any formal education in business. Because you are a gatherer of information, especially when it has to do with information needed to apply to your clients and businesses, you naturally develop what I call uncanny "business smarts." Using your common sense, collection of resources and love of learning, you can create a successful entrepreneurial business. And because you are a lifelong learner, you continue to seek new information to keep your businesses thriving. Bottom line...never stop learning! It is a huge secret to your success!

Curious

"When you're curious, you find lots of interesting things to do."

~ Walt Disney

Curious

Curiosity is the instinctive desire to ask questions. Where would our world be without this amazing quality that is characteristic of persons with entrepreneurial brain styles? Curiosity opens you up to learning, understanding and creating.

As someone with an entrepreneurial brain style, curiosity has you always asking "why," "what," "how" or "when" and has resulted in many marvelous technological, medical, business and geographic advances in our world.

Your inherent curiosity helps you really understand your clients and your market niche. Curiosity helps you understand how to serve them, what products would be the most valuable for them. Curiosity has you wondering about your mistakes so that you can learn from them and try new things!

As an entrepreneur, curiosity has you paying attention to how others are serving your market and ideal client. Curiosity helps you learn what will work to reach them and what won't. Below are a few well-known entrepreneurs...no doubt with curious entrepreneurial brain styles like yours!

- Benjamin Franklin
- Thomas Edison
- P.T. Barnum
- Henry Ford
- Steve Jobs
- Jack Dorsey
- Bill Gates

Not Afraid to Make a Mistake

"As you begin to take action toward the fulfillment of your goals and dreams, you must realize that not every action will be perfect. Not every action will produce the desired result. Not every action will work. Making mistakes, getting it almost right, and experimenting to see what happens are all part of the process of eventually getting it right."

~ Jack Canfield

Not Afraid to Make a Mistake

A key secret of creating a profitable and productive business for you with entrepreneurial brain styles is that you are less afraid of making mistakes - because you see them not as failures but rather as an opportunity to learn and improve. In fact, many with entrepreneurial brain styles don't even recognize "mistakes" or "failures" because it is assumed these were all part of the process of improving their ability to serve.

You are more comfortable taking risks, trying things for the first time and maybe even having them not work out. You don't focus on blame or retribution, and instead work on finding solutions to rectify "what didn't work" and prevent it from happening again. In general, those like you blessed with an entrepreneurial brain style, are not afraid of making a mistake because there are no mistakes, just opportunities to adjust your path and improve.

Fly By the Seat of Your Pants

"The most difficult thing is the decision to act, the rest is merely tenacity. The fears are paper tigers. You can do anything you decide to do. You can act to change and control your life; and the procedure, the process is its own reward."

~ Amelia Earhart

Fly By the Seat of Your Pants

The term, "flying by the seat of their pants" emerged in the 1930's during WWII when pilots would have to navigate their planes without a radio or compass to guide them. Without these to steer them, pilots would have to make changes and course corrections using their own initiative, intuition and instincts. They thrived in these uncertain conditions. You, with an entrepreneurial brain style, also have this gift.

If it's true that the only thing certain in business is that it is uncertain, being able to "fly by the seat of your pants" is indeed a key to your success. You have access to this same talent to adjust your course in order to keep on top of your industry. Using your intuition, you can always be ready to change if you see a new opportunity arise.

Successful entrepreneurs are always on their toes, ready to make shifts if needed. Undoubtedly, your business will have its ups and downs, and with your entrepreneurial brain style, you have the ability to make necessary course corrections and reach your goals via "flying by the seat of your pants."

Resilient

"Your time is limited, so don't waste it living someone else's life. Don't be trapped by dogma – which is living with the results of other people's thinking. Don't let the noise of other's opinions drown out your own inner voice. Most importantly, have the courage to follow your heart and intuition. They somehow already know what you truly want to become. Everything else is secondary."

~ Steve Jobs

Resilient

Being an entrepreneur means you will be working countless hours and perhaps making many sacrifices to make your business a success. You will start early, stay late, work weekends and holidays. Luckily, you with your entrepreneurial brain style, have an almost super-human quality that makes it possible for you to bounce back time and again. To get out of bed the next day and start over if needed. It is called being "resilient." Webster's dictionary defines resiliency as: leaping back; rebounding; recoiling, and you have this in abundance!

Running your own business and being an entrepreneur requires the ability to manage chaos, unpredictability and inconsistency (a.k.a. stress). You, with your entrepreneurial brain style and your high interest and tolerance for the new and stimulating, are often at your best in what otherwise would be a crisis situation. In fact, your ability to tolerate and adapt to uncertainty lead to the exact situations where you might have noticed that you tend to be most focused and clear headed. Without this resiliency, you would literally crack, mentally or physically, under the pressure.

However, having this resilience doesn't mean that you can stop taking care of yourself physically and mentally with exercise, diet and sleep. Even super humans need to have people and support systems in their lives to help them through the rough patches and celebrate successes. Don't forget what Hans Selye said, "Stress is not what happens to us. It's our response TO what happens. And RESPONSE is something we can choose."

In parting, I want to leave you with this final thought:

Having an entrepreneurial brain style means that you have been gifted with innumerable abilities and talents that add to your natural ability to be successful as an entrepreneur. Sometimes, having so many amazing qualities might not leave room for some of the more mundane pieces of business such as time management, planning, or organizing. But, this is the great news! You can learn and become competent in these other key areas of entrepreneurship so that they do not get in the way of your reaching your service, productivity or profitability goals. By working with your amazing entrepreneurial brain and learning new strategies and techniques to better manage areas where there are challenges, you will enjoy the full potential of your business and your life.

Blessings,

Laurie

Want to find out more about Unlocking the Secrets to your Entrepreneurial Brain Style and how you can open your business to productivity and profitability?

Visit Laurie at:

www.CoachingforADHD.com

Want to talk with others who have entrepreneurial brains like yours? Visit and "like" me on Facebook at:

www.facebook.com/CoachingforADHD

Work directly with Laurie Dupar

Schedule a 15-minute consultation with Laurie today to find out how you can unlock the secrets of your entrepreneurial brain style and reach the service, productivity and profitability goals for your business.

Go to:
www.CoachingforADHD.com

or email:

Laurie@CoachingforADHD.com

I look forward to hearing from you!

~Laurie

Made in the USA
Charleston, SC
17 March 2012